First Facts

CURIOUS SCIENTISTS

AMAZING LIFE SCIENCE ACTIVITIES

by Rani Iyer

CAPSTONE PRESS
a capstone imprint

First Facts are published by Capstone Press,
1710 Roe Crest Drive, North Mankato, Minnesota 56003
www.mycapstone.com

Library of Congress Cataloging-in-Publication Data
Cataloging-in-publication information is on file with the Library of Congress.
ISBN 978-1-5157-6886-9 (library binding)
ISBN 978-1-5157-6892-0 (paperback)
ISBN 978-1-5157-6904-0 (eBook PDF)

Editorial Credits
Anna Butzer, editor; Heidi Thompson, designer; Morgan Walters, media researcher; Kathy McColley, production specialist

Photo Credits
All photos shot by Capstone Studio, Karon Dubke; Shutterstock: amgun, Cover, design element throughout, FRDMR, left 18, greenazya, 21, Robyn Mackenzie, right 18

Printed and bound in the USA.
010374F17

TABLE OF CONTENTS

CURIOUS LIFE

Do you wonder about the plants and animals living in the world around you? Do you ask questions about life cycles? Can something be both living and nonliving? To find out the answers to questions like these, curious scientists do experiments.

Now it's your turn to be a curious scientist. Get ready to use your creativity and get a little messy! You will find out what it's like to eat like a bird and discover how frogs stay warm in cold weather. The results of your experiments will be amazing!

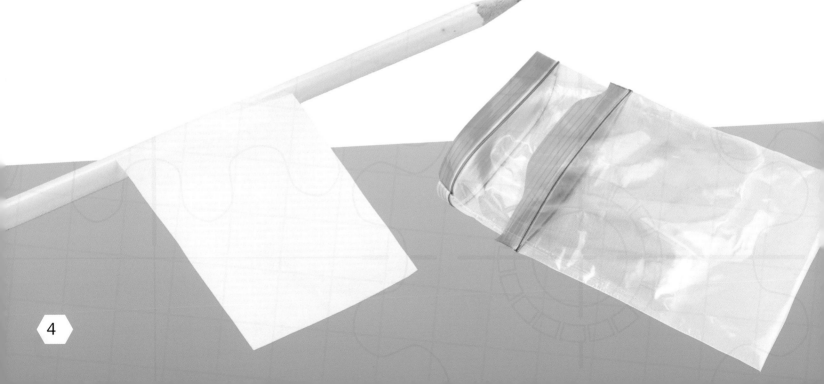

Safe Science

Read through each activity before
starting. Collect all of the materials that
you will need. You may need an adult
to help you find or buy some materials.
Experiments can be tricky. Be sure to
ask an adult for help if you need it.

WATCH SEEDS SPROUT

Ever wonder what happens after you plant a seed in the ground? This experiment will show you what is going on underground! Watch seeds **germinate** before your eyes. Then see your plants grow each day.

Materials:

- water
- 1-2 paper towels
- Mason jar
- 2-3 seeds (sunflower, popcorn, peas, or beans)

Steps:

1. Dampen two to three paper towels. Ring out the paper towels so no excess water sits in the jar. Place the paper towels in the mason jar.
2. Place the seeds in the jar. Position them in different places inside the jar toward the outside so you can see them.
3. Place the jar near a window that gets plenty of sunlight.
4. Check back after a couple of days. What do you see?

Step 2

How it Works:

All seeds need moisture, clean air, and the right temperature to germinate. With the right conditions the plant inside starts to grow and get bigger. Moisture comes from the wet paper towels. The right temperature is created when the jar is placed near a window that gets sunlight. Clean air is also inside the jar. All the things needed for the seeds to germinate are inside the jar. It breaks out of the seed coat. Roots reach down, and a **shoot** grows up. After about five to six days, take your growing plants out and place them in dirt. Growing plants need the nutrients from soil and sunlight to survive.

germinate—when a seed sends out a root and a stem

shoot—the white stem growing out of a seed that becomes a plant

STAYING WARM IN THE ARCTIC

The Arctic is a **frigid** place on Earth. Many animals live on land and in the freezing water. Polar bears, whales, harp seals, and walruses are some animals that live in the Arctic. In this activity, you will discover how these animals stay warm in cold **climates**.

Materials:

- 4 plastic zip-top bags
- vegetable shortening
- spoon
- large bowl
- ice cubes
- water
- stopwatch
- paper and pencil

Steps:

1. Turn one of the zip-top bags inside out and place it in another bag. Line the zip-tops up so you can zip the bags together.

2. Using the spoon, put about 1½ cups (285 grams) of shortening in between the two bags. Spread the shortening around to create a layer between the two bags. Zip the bags together.

3. Do the same thing with the other two zip-top bags, but don't add the shortening.

4. Fill a large bowl with ice cubes and water. It should be deep enough for your hands to be fully underwater.

5. Put your hand in the plain zip-top bag, and put it in the ice water. Use the stopwatch to time how long you can keep your hand in before it gets too cold.

Step 1

6. Remove your hands when you get uncomfortable. Stop your stopwatch, and write down the time.
7. Now put the same hand in the zip-top bag with the layer of shortening. Put it in the ice water. Use the stopwatch again to time how long you can keep it in the water. Record your results.
8. Look at your data. Were you able to keep your hand in the ice water longer using the zip-top bag with the layer of shortening? What was the time difference?

How it Works:

Animals living in cold places develop several **adaptations** to live in their climate. One adaptation is to develop a layer of fat under the skin called blubber. The fat keeps the animal's body insulated in cold climates. Shortening is a type of fat. When you added shortening to the zip-top bags, you protected your hand from the cold. Therefore, you were able to keep your hand in cold water for a longer time.

frigid—very cold in temperature

climate—the usual weather that occurs in a place

adaptation—a change a living thing goes through to better fit in with its environment

A FROG'S TRICK TO SURVIVING WINTER

In winter, you might bundle up with a winter jacket, a hat, and mittens. But some frogs use what they have inside their bodies to stay warm. In this experiment, you will discover the chemicals that frogs use to keep from freezing.

Materials:

- two small, clear freezer-safe containers with lids
- 1 cup (236 milliliters) water
- kitchen scale
- paper and pencil
- 1 cup (236 ml) maple syrup
- freezer
- bowl

Steps:

1. Pour the water into one of the containers. Place the container on the scale. How much does it weigh? Write it down. Put the lid on tight.
2. Pour the maple syrup into the other container. Place on the kitchen scale. Write down the weight. Snap the lid on tightly.
3. Put the two containers in the freezer.
4. Wait 5 to 6 hours.
5. Remove the containers carefully from the freezer.
6. Place the water container on the kitchen scale. Has the weight changed? Do the same with the syrup.

Step 2

7.	Which is heavier? Was the container with water heavier after you froze it?

8.	Open the container with water. Are you able to pour it into the bowl? Is the water frozen? Set the container aside.

9.	Open the container with syrup. Does the syrup pour into the bowl?

10.	What does the syrup contain that the water does not have? Taste the syrup and water to find out the difference.

How it Works:

Animal cells have water. If the cells freeze, the animal can die. Freezing increases weight and causes water to expand. During winter some frogs produce a lot of a type of sugar called **glucose**. It keeps their blood from freezing. Even when the outside of the frog's body freezes, the cells remain alive due to glucose. In this experiment, it was the sugar in the maple syrup that kept it from freezing.

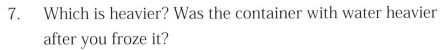

glucose—a natural sugar that gives energy to living things

EAT LIKE A BIRD

Every bird has a certain way of eating. Hummingbirds have a beak that is long and thin. This helps it dip into flowers to sip nectar. An eagle swoops on its **prey** in the air or dives to the ground to pick it up. In this activity, you will learn how birds' adaptations help them survive.

Materials:

Food

- marshmallows
- salad leaves
- rice
- peanuts in shell or pistachios in shell
- juice
- paper and pencil

Bird beaks

- tweezers
- chopsticks
- tongs
- pliers
- straw

Steps:

1. Arrange the food in an orderly manner.
2. Write down the order in which they are all arranged.
3. Use each of the "beak" items to pick up the food.
4. Write down or describe what happens when you pick up the food with one of the "beak" items.

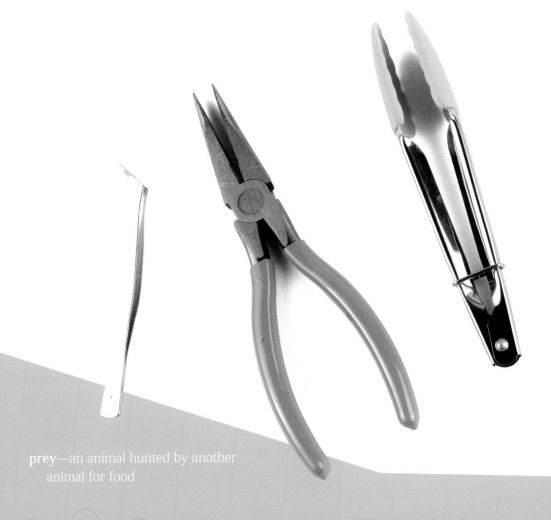

prey—an animal hunted by another animal for food

Examples of what you might observe:

- It is hard to use chopsticks to break open the shells of nuts.
- The tongs are too big to pick up pieces of rice.
- It is easy to crack open the nuts with the pliers.

Now list the other things you observed.

How it Works:

Different birds have different beaks. They come in many shapes and sizes. All birds have specialized beaks that help them find food and eat in the place they live. The place they live is called a **habitat**. Woodpeckers have a tweezer-like beak. They can peck holes in dead trees and grab the tiny insects living inside. The pliers are like the powerful beak of a cardinal. They crack open pistachio nuts.

CACTUS SURVIVAL

Have you ever forgotten to water a plant and it started to die? Plants need water to survive! But cactuses are known for living in desert climates. In this activity you'll discover how a cactus can live in such a hot and dry place.

Materials:

- marker
- scissors
- 2 sponges
- paper and pencil
- measuring cup
- water
- 2 plastic cups
- kitchen scale
- cookie sheet
- wax paper

Steps:

1. Draw the shape of a cactus on one of the sponges. Cut it out.
2. Place it on top of the second sponge and trace around it. Cut out the second sponge cactus. This way the sponges will be about the same size. Weigh each sponge and record the weight.
3. Put 1/3 cup (79 ml) of water in each plastic cup. Place a sponge cactus into each cup and set aside for one hour.

4. Remove each sponge and weigh it. Write down your observations.
5. Set the cactus sponges onto the cookie sheet. Wrap one of the sponges with a sheet of wax paper.
6. Check on your cactus sponges for a few days. Weigh the sponges each day. Which sponge dried out faster?

How it Works:

Cactuses go through a process called **photosynthesis** just like other plants. They need the sun for energy. They also need water to survive. But how do cactuses that live in the desert survive during long periods of time without any water? They have adapted to their environment. Cactuses store water inside and save it for later. The waxy coating of a cactus helps keep the water from **evaporating**. Similarly, the waxed paper helped the sponge hold moisture.

photosynthesis—process by which plants make food using sunlight, carbon dioxide, and water

evaporate—process of change in water from a liquid to a gas

THE CHANGING COLORS OF LEAVES

You know that summer is over and fall is starting when the leaves on trees begin to change. Green leaves turn orange, red, yellow, and brown. This easy **chromatography** activity will show you how to find the hidden colors in leaves.

Materials:

- several leaves from 2-3 different trees, found on the ground
- 2-3 small glasses or jars with lids
- spoon
- rubbing alcohol
- dish
- hot water
- scissors
- white paper coffee filters
- tape
- pencil

Steps:

1. Tear the leaves into pieces and place them in the jars. Use the back of the spoon to crush the leaves up even more.
2. Pour just enough rubbing alcohol into the jars to cover the leaves.
3. Cover the jars with their lids (or plastic wrap) to keep the alcohol from evaporating.
4. Put the jars in a dish of hot tap water. Let them sit for about 30 minutes or until the alcohol turns green.

Tip: Keep leaves from different trees separate as you collect them.

5. Cut a few strips of filter paper about 2 inches (5 cm) wide. Tape the strips to a pencil.

6. Uncover the jars and set the pencil across. Let the strip just barely touch the alcohol mixture.

7. Let the filter strips sit in the mixture for at least two hours.

8. Take them out and let them dry.

How it Works:

Plants use photosynthesis to convert the sun's rays into food. To absorb the light, leaves use their brightly colored **pigments**. Even though a leaf looks like it is mostly one color, it actually has different pigments that you can't see. The most important pigment is **chlorophyll**. In the fall, the chlorophyll begins to break down. That is when we start to see the leaves changing color. What are the different bands of colors on the filter strips? These are the different pigments in the leaves. This experiment will help you predict what color the leaves will be in the fall.

chromatography—a process for separating different components from a mixture

pigment—a substance that gives something a particular color when it is present in it or is added to it

chlorophyll— the green substance in plants that uses light to make food from carbon dioxide and water

19

MOLDY BREAD

It's lunchtime. You sit down and are about to start eating. Wait! Did you wash your hands? Your skin is home to billions of **bacteria**. But when your hands don't look dirty it is easy to forget about the bacteria you can't see. This activity will show you how quickly bacteria grows.

Materials:

- three zip-top sandwich bags
- permanent marker
- tongs or disposable gloves
- three slices of wheat bread
- water in a spray bottle
- soap and water for hand washing
- paper towel

Steps:

1. Use the permanent marker to label the zip-top bags. Label them "not touched", "dirty hands", and "clean hands."
2. Use the tongs or gloves to take one slice of bread and put it inside the zip-top bag labeled "not touched." Make sure you don't touch the bread or the inside of the bag with your fingers!
3. Spray the bread with two sprays of water and seal the bag.
4. Take the next slice of bread and touch it with your bare hands. Put the bread inside the bag labeled "dirty hands." Spray the bread with two sprays of water and seal the bag.

5. Wash your hands with soap and water and dry them with a paper towel. Take the last slice of bread and put it in the bag labeled "clean hands." Spray the bread twice and seal the bag.

6. Check the bags for the next 6 to 7 days. What do you see?

How it Works:

Mold will grow on all three slices, but more mold will appear sooner on the slice that you touched before you washed your hands. Mold is a tiny, living **organism** that gets its energy from the material on which it grows. Mold is able to grow on objects that have small amounts of living material. The mold grew quicker on the slice that was touched with dirty hands because of the bacteria on it.

Not Touched

Clean Hands

Dirty Hands

bacteria—one-celled, tiny living things; some are helpful and some cause disease

organism—a living thing such as a plant, animal, bacterium, or fungus

GLOSSARY

adaptation (a-dap-TAY-shuhn)—a change a living thing goes through to better fit in with its environment

bacteria (bak-TEER-ee-uh)—one celled, tiny living things; some are helpful and some cause disease

chromatography (kro-mah-TOG-ruh-fee)—a process for separating different components from a mixture

chlorophyll (KLOR-uh-fil)—the green substance in plants that uses light to make food from carbon dioxide and water

climate (KLY-muht)—the usual weather that occurs in a place

evaporate (i-VA-puh-rayt)—process of change in water from a liquid to a gas

frigid (FRIJ-id)—very cold in temperature

glucose (GLOO-kose)—a natural sugar that gives energy to living things

germinate (JUR-muh-nayt)—when a seed sends out a root and a stem

habitat (HAB-uh-tat)—the natural place and conditions in which a plant or animal lives

organism (OR-guh-niz-uhm)—a living thing such as a plant, animal, bacterium, or fungus

photosynthesis (foh-toh-SIN-thuh-siss)—process by which plants make food using sunlight, carbon dioxide, and water

pigment (PIG-ment)—a substance that gives something a particular color when it is present in it or is added to it

prey (PRAY)—an animal hunted by another animal for food

shoot (SHOOT)—the white stem growing out of a seed that becomes a plant

READ MORE

Canavan, Thomas. *Awesome Experiments with Living Things.* Mind-Blowing Science Experiments. New York: Gareth Stevens Pub., 2017.

Gardner, Robert. *Experiments for Future Biologists.* Experiments for Future Stem Professionals. New York: Enslow Publishing, 2016.

Thomas, Isabel. *Experiments with Plants.* Read and Experiment. Chicago: Heinemann Raintree, 2016.

INTERNET SITES

Use FactHound to find Internet sites related to this book:

Visit *www.facthound.com*

Just type in 9781515768869 and go.

 Super-cool stuff! Check out projects, games and lots more at **www.capstonekids.com**

INDEX